The Half-Inch Himalayas

. . . for wherever I seat
myself, I die in exile.
— Virginia Woolf

Wesleyan New Poets

Agha Shahid Ali

The Half-Inch Himalayas

Wesleyan University Press

For Sufia & Ashraf

WESLEYAN UNIVERSITY PRESS
Published by University Press of New England, Hanover, NH 03755
© 1987 by Agha Shahid Ali

Printed in the United States of America   5   4

The writing of this book has been supported by a grant from The
Commonwealth of Pennsylvania Council on the Arts.

Some of these poems appeared originally in *The Agni Review, Ascent, The
Beloit Poetry Journal, Chandrabhaga, The Chariton Review, Cimarron
Review, Crazyhorse, The Fiddlehead, How Strong the Roots, Intro #9,
Journal of General Education, Kunapipi, Pivot, Poem, Quarterly West,
Shenandoah, Willow Springs,* and *Xanadu.*

LIBRARY OF CONGRESS CATALOGING-IN-PUBLICATION DATA
Agha, Shahid Ali
     The half-inch Himalayas.
     (Wesleyan new poets)
     I. Title. II. Series.
PR9499.3.A39H3   1987   821   86-9183
ISBN 0-8195-2131-0 (alk. paper)
ISBN 0-8195-1132-3 (pbk.: alk. paper)

Contents

Postcard from Kashmir

Kashmir shrinks into my mailbox,
my home a neat four by six inches.

I always loved neatness. Now I hold
the half-inch Himalayas in my hand.

This is home. And this the closest
I'll ever be to home. When I return,
the colors won't be so brilliant,
the Jhelum's waters so clean,
so ultramarine. My love
so overexposed.

And my memory will be a little
out of focus, in it
a giant negative, black
and white, still undeveloped.

(for Pavan Sahgal)

I

A Lost Memory of Delhi

I am not born
it is 1948 and the bus turns
onto a road without name

There on his bicycle
my father
He is younger than I

At Okhla where I get off
I pass my parents
strolling by the Jamuna River

My mother is a recent bride
her sari a blaze of brocade
Silverdust parts her hair

She doesn't see me
The bells of her anklets are distant
like the sound of china from

teashops being lit up with lanterns
and the stars are coming out
ringing with tongues of glass

They go into the house
always faded in photographs
in the family album

but lit up now
with the oil lamp
I saw broken in the attic

I want to tell them I am their son
older much older than they are
I knock keep knocking

but for them the night is quiet
this the night of my being
They don't they won't

hear me they won't hear
my knocking drowning out
the tongues of stars

A Dream of Glass Bangles

Those autumns my parents slept
warm in a quilt studded
with pieces of mirrors

On my mother's arms were bangles
like waves of frozen rivers
and at night

after the prayers
as she went down to her room
I heard the faint sound of ice

breaking on the staircase
breaking years later
into winter

our house surrounded by men
pulling icicles for torches
off the roofs

rubbing them on the walls
till the cement's darkening red
set the tips of water on fire

the air a quicksand of snow
as my father stepped out
and my mother

inside the burning house
a widow smashing the rivers
on her arms

Snowmen

My ancestor, a man
of Himalayan snow,
came to Kashmir from Samarkand,
carrying a bag
of whale bones:
heirlooms from sea funerals.
His skeleton
carved from glaciers, his breath
arctic,
he froze women in his embrace.
His wife thawed into stony water,
her old age a clear
evaporation.

This heirloom,
his skeleton under my skin, passed
from son to grandson,
generations of snowmen on my back.
They tap every year on my window,
their voices hushed to ice.

No, they won't let me out of winter,
and I've promised myself,
even if I'm the last snowman,
that I'll ride into spring
on their melting shoulders.

Cracked Portraits

My grandfather's painted grandfather,
son of Ali, a strange physician
in embroidered robes, a white turban,
the Koran lying open on a table beside him.

I look for prayers
in his eyes, for inscriptions
in Arabic.
I find his will:
He's left us plots
in the family graveyard.

     ✿   ✿   ✿

Great-grandfather? A sahib in breeches.
He simply disappoints me,
his hands missing in the drawing-room photo
but firm as he whipped the horses
or the servants.

He wound the gramophone to a fury,
the needles grazing Malika Pukhraj's songs
as he, drunk, tore his shirts
and wept at the refrain,
"I still am young."

     ✿   ✿   ✿

Grandfather, a handsome boy,
sauntered toward madness
into Srinagar's interior.
In a dim-lit shop he smoked hashish,
reciting verses of Sufi mystics.
My father went to bring him home.

As he grew older, he moved toward Plato,
mumbling "philosopher-king,"

Napoleon on his lips.
Sitting in the bedroom corner,
smoking his hookah, he told me
the Siberian snows
froze the French bones.

In his cup,
Socrates swirled.

    ❋   ❋   ❋

I turn the pages,
see my father holding a tennis racquet,
ready to score with women,
brilliance clinging to his shirt.

He brings me closer to myself
as he quotes Lenin's love of Beethoven,
but loses me as he turns to Gandhi.

Silverfish have eaten his boyhood face.

    ❋   ❋   ❋

Cobwebs cling
to the soundless
words of my ancestors.

No one now comes from Kandahar,
dear Ali, to pitch tents by the Jhelum,
under autumn maples,
and claim descent from the holy prophet.

Your portrait is desolate
in a creaking corridor.

(for Agha Zafar Ali)

10

Story of a Silence

While her husband
thumbed through Plato, spending
the dialogues

like a pension,
in whispers, his inheritance lost,
his house

taken away,
my grandmother worked hard, harder
than a man

to earn
her salary from the government and
deserve

her heirloom
of prayer from God. When he slept,
she leafed

through
his dreams: she wasn't in any
of them

and he
was just lying on the river's warm
glass, thousands

of him
moving under him. He was nothing
when he woke,

only his own
duplicates in her arms. Years later
she went

into the night,
in one hand the Koran, in the other
a minaret

of fire. She
found him sleeping, his torn Plato, his
pillow, the fire's

light a cold
quilt on him. She held him as only
a shadow must

be held. But
then the darkness cracked, and
he was gone.

Prayer Rug

Those intervals
between the day's
five calls to prayer

the women of the house
pulling thick threads
through vegetables

rosaries of ginger
of rustling peppers
in autumn drying for winter

in those intervals this rug
part of Grandma's dowry
folded

so the Devil's shadow
would not desecrate
Mecca scarlet-woven

with minarets of gold
but then the sunset
call to prayer

the servants
their straw mats unrolled
praying or in the garden

in summer on grass
the children wanting
the prayers to end

the women's foreheads
touching Abraham's
silk stone of sacrifice

black stone descended
from Heaven
the pilgrims in white circling it

this year my grandmother
also a pilgrim
in Mecca she weeps

as the stone is unveiled
she weeps holding on
to the pillars

(for Begum Zafar Ali)

The Dacca Gauzes

. . . for a whole year he sought
to accumulate the most exquisite
Dacca gauzes.
    — Oscar Wilde/*The Picture of
        Dorian Gray*

Those transparent Dacca gauzes
known as woven air, running
water, evening dew:

a dead art now, dead over
a hundred years. "No one
now knows," my grandmother says,

"what it was to wear
or touch that cloth." She wore
it once, an heirloom sari from

her mother's dowry, proved
genuine when it was pulled, all
six yards, through a ring.

Years later when it tore,
many handkerchiefs embroidered
with gold-thread paisleys

were distributed among
the nieces and daughters-in-law.
Those too now lost.

In history we learned: the hands
of weavers were amputated,
the looms of Bengal silenced,

and the cotton shipped raw
by the British to England.
History of little use to her,

my grandmother just says
how the muslins of today
seem so coarse and that only

in autumn, should one wake up
at dawn to pray, can one
feel that same texture again.

One morning, she says, the air
was dew-starched: she pulled
it absently through her ring.

The Season of the Plains

In Kashmir, where the year
has four, clear seasons, my mother
spoke of her childhood

in the plains of Lucknow, and
of that season in itself,
the monsoon, when Krishna's

flute is heard on the shores
of the Jamuna. She played old records
of the Banaras thumri-singers,

Siddheshwari and Rasoolan, their
voices longing, when the clouds
gather, for that invisible

blue god. Separation
can't be borne when the rains
come: this every lyric says.

While children run out
into the alleys, soaking
their utter summer,

messages pass between lovers.
Heer and Ranjha and others
of legends, their love forbidden,

burned incense all night,
waiting for answers. My mother
hummed Heer's lament

but never told me if she
also burned sticks
of jasmine that, dying,

kept raising soft necks
of ash. I imagined
each neck leaning

on the humid air. She only
said: The monsoons never cross
the mountains into Kashmir.

II

A Monsoon Note on Old Age

This is fifty years later: I
sit across myself, folded in
monsoon sweat, my skin

shriveled, a tired eunuch, aware
only of an absence;
                          the window bars

sketch a prison on me;
                          I shuffle the stars,
a pack of old cards;

                    the night regains
its textures of rain. I overexpose
your photograph, dusting

death's far-off country.

A Butcher

In this lane
near Jama Masjid,

where he wraps kilos of meat
in sheets of paper,

the ink of the news
stains his knuckles,

the script is wet
in his palms: Urdu,

bloody at his fingertips,
is still fine on his lips,

the language polished smooth
by knives

on knives. He hacks
the festival goats, throws

their skins to dogs.
I smile and quote

a Ghalib line; he completes
the couplet, smiles,

quotes a Mir line. I complete
the couplet.

He wraps my kilo of ribs.
I give him the money. The change

clutters our moment of courtesy,
our phrases snapping in mid-syllable,

Ghalib's ghazals left unrhymed.

Note: Jama Masjid is the great mosque of Delhi. Ghalib and
    Mir, two of the greatest Urdu poets, are especially known
    for their ghazals.

The Fate of the Astrologer Sitting on the Pavement Outside the Delhi Railway Station

"Pay, pay attention to the sky,"
he shouts to passers-by.

The planets gather dust
from passing trucks.

After Seeing Kozintsev's
King Lear in Delhi

Lear cries out "You are men of stones"
as Cordelia hangs from a broken wall.

I step out into Chandni Chowk, a street once
strewn with jasmine flowers
for the Empress and the royal women
who bought perfumes from Isfahan,
fabrics from Dacca, essence from Kabul,
glass bangles from Agra.

Beggars now live here in tombs
of unknown nobles and forgotten saints
while hawkers sell combs and mirrors
outside a Sikh temple. Across the street,
a theater is showing a Bombay spectacular.

I think of Zafar, poet and Emperor,
being led through this street
by British soldiers, his feet in chains,
to watch his sons hanged.

In exile he wrote:
"Unfortunate Zafar
spent half his life in hope,
the other half waiting.
He begs for two yards of Delhi for burial."

He was exiled to Burma, buried in Rangoon.

Chandni Chowk, Delhi

Swallow this summer street,
then wait for the monsoon.
Needles of rain

melt on the tongue. Will you go
farther? A memory of drought
holds you: you remember

the taste of hungry words
and you chew syllables of salt.

Can you rinse away this city that lasts
like blood on the bitten tongue?

Cremation

Your bones refused to burn
when we set fire to the flesh.

Who would have guessed
you'd be stubborn in death?

In Memory of Begum Akhtar
(∂. 30 October 1974)

1

Your death in every paper,
boxed in the black and white
of photographs, obituaries,

the sky warm, blue, ordinary,
no hint of calamity,

no room for sobs,
even between the lines.

I wish to talk of the end of the world.

2

Do your fingers still scale the hungry
Bhairavi, or simply the muddy shroud?

Ghazal, that death-sustaining widow,
sobs in dingy archives, hooked to you.
She wears her grief, a moon-soaked white,
corners the sky into disbelief.

You've finally polished catastrophe,
the note you seasoned with decades
of Ghalib, Mir, Faiz:

I innovate on a noteless raga.

3

Exiling you to cold mud,
your coffin, stupid and white,
astounds by its ignorance.

It wears its blank pride,
defleshing the nomad's echo.
I follow you to the earth's claw,

shouldering time's shadow.
This is history's bitter arrogance,
this moment of the bone's freedom.

 4

You cannot cross-examine the dead.

I've taken the circumstantial evidence,
your records, pictures, tapes, and
offered a careless testimony.

I wish to summon you in defense,
but the grave's damp and cold, now when
Malhar longs to stitch the rain,

wrap you in its notes: you elude
completely. The rain doesn't speak,
and life, once again, closes in,

reasserting this earth where the air
meets in a season of grief.

(for Saleem Kidwai)

Homage to Faiz Ahmed Faiz
(∂. 20 November 1984)

"You are welcome to make your
adaptations of my poems."

1

You wrote this from Beirut, two years before
the Sabra-Shatila massacres. That city's
refugee air was open, torn
by jets and the voices of reporters.
As always, you were witness to "rains of stones,"

though you were away from Pakistan, from
the laws of home which said: the hands
of thieves will be surgically
amputated. But the subcontinent always spoke
to you: in Ghalib's Urdu, and sometimes through

the old masters who sang of twilight
but didn't live, like Ghalib, to see the wind
rip the collars of the dawn: the summer
of 1857, the trees of Delhi
became scaffolds: 30,000 men

were hanged. Wherever you were, Faiz, that
language spoke to you; and when you heard it,
you were alone — in Tunis, Beirut,
London, or Moscow. Those poets' laments
concealed, as yours revealed, the sorrows

of a broken time. You knew Ghalib was right:
blood must not merely follow routine, must not
just flow as the veins' uninterrupted
river. Sometimes it must flood the eyes,
surprise them by being clear as water.

2

I didn't listen when my father
recited your poems to us
by heart. What could it mean to a boy

that you had redefined the cruel
beloved, that figure who already
was Friend, Woman, God? In your hands

she was Revolution. You gave
her silver hands, her lips were red.
Impoverished lovers waited all

night every night, but she remained
only a glimpse behind
light. When I learned of her,

I was no longer a boy, and Urdu
a silhouette traced
by the voices of singers,

by Begum Akhtar, who wove your couplets
into ragas: both language and music
were sharpened. I listened:

and you became, like memory,
necessary. *Dast-e-Saba,*
I said to myself. And quietly

the wind opened its palms: I read
there of the night: the secrets
of lovers, the secrets of prisons.

3

When you permitted my hands to turn to stone,
as must happen to a translator's hands,

I thought of you writing *Zindan-Nama*
on prison walls, on cigarette packages,

on torn envelopes. Your lines were measured
so carefully to become in our veins

the blood of prisoners. In the free verse
of another language I imprisoned

each line — but I touched my own exile.
This hush, while your ghazals lay in my palms,

was accurate, as is this hush that falls
at news of your death over Pakistan

and India and over all of us no
longer there to whom you spoke in Urdu.

Twenty days before your death you finally
wrote, this time from Lahore, that after the sack

of Beirut you had no address . . . I
had gone from poem to poem, and found

you once, terribly alone, speaking
to yourself: "Bolt your doors, Sad heart! Put out

the candles, break all cups of wine. No one,
now no one will ever return." But you

still waited, Faiz, for that God, that Woman,
that Friend, that Revolution, to come

at last. And because you waited,
I listen as you pass with some song,

a memory of musk, the rebel face of hope.

III

A Wrong Turn

In my dream I'm always
in a massacred town, its name
erased from maps,
no road signs to it.
Only a wrong turn brings me here

where only the noon sun lives.
I'm alone, walking among the atrocities,
guillotines blood-scorched,
gods stabbed at their altars,
dry wells piled up with bones,
a curfew on ghosts.

Who were these people?
And who finished them to the last?
If dust had an alphabet, I would learn.

I thrust my hand
into the cobwebbed booth
of the town's ghost station,
the platform a snake-scaled rock,
rusted tracks waiting for a lost train,
my ticket a dead spider
hard as stone.

Vacating an Apartment

1

Efficient as Fate,
each eye a storm trooper,

the cleaners wipe my smile
with Comet fingers
and tear the plaster
off my suicide note.

They learn everything
from the walls' eloquent tongues.

Now, quick as genocide,
they powder my ghost for a cinnamon jar.

They burn my posters
(India and Heaven in flames),

whitewash my voicestains,

make everything new,
clean as Death.

2

When the landlord brings new tenants,
even Memory is a stranger.

The woman, her womb solid with the future,
instructs her husband's eyes
to clutch insurance policies.

They ignore my love affair with the furniture,
the corner table that memorized
my crossed-out lines.

Oh, she's beautiful,
a hard-nippled Madonna.

The landlord gives them my autopsy;
they sign the lease.

The room is beating with bottled infants,
and I've stopped beating.

I'm moving out holding tombstones in my hands.

The Previous Occupant

The landlady says he lived here
for years. There's enough missing
for me to know him. On the empty shelves,
absent books gather dust: Neruda. Cavafy.
I know he knew their poetry, by heart
the lines I love.

From a half-torn horoscope I learn
his sign: Aquarius, just like me.
A half-empty Flexsol in the cabinet:
he wore soft lenses. Yes, Aquarians are vain.
And no anthems on their lips, they travel
great distances. He came from some country
as far as Chile.

She says the apartment
will be cleaned by the 1st:

But no detergent will rub his voice from the air
though he has disappeared in some country
as far as Chile.
The stains of his thoughts still cling
in phrases to the frost on the windows.

And though he is blinded in some prison,
though he is dying in some country
as far as Chile,
no spray will get inside the mirror
from where his brown eyes,
brown, yes, brown,
stare as if for years he'd been
searching for me.

Now that he's found me,
my body casts his shadow everywhere.
He'll never, never, move out of here.

Leaving Your City

In the midnight bar
your breath collapsed on me.
I balanced on

the tip of your smile,

holding on to your words
as I climbed the dark steps.

Meticulous,
your furniture neatly arranged for death,

you sharpened the knife
on the moon's surface,
polished it with lunatic silver.

You were kind,
reciting poetry in a drunk tongue.
I thought: At last!

Now I loiter in and out
of your memory,

speaking to you wherever I go.

I'm reduced to my poverties

and you to a restless dream
from another country

where the sea is the most expensive blue.

✿   ✿   ✿

My finger, your phone number
at its tip, dials the night.

And your city follows me,
its lights dying in my eyes.

Philadelphia, 2:00 A.M.

All routes to death
will open up, again,
as the bars close all over
Pennsylvania:

The disco stills its lights.
My eyes dim,
            then go off

in the mirrors;
            I swallow
the melting rocks in my glass,

looking for shortcuts
by-passing death,

my skin tense with
the taxi-hour of loss.

(for Howard Motyl)

The Jogger on
Riverside Drive, 5:00 A.M.

The dark scissors of his legs
cut the moon's

raw silk, highways of wind
torn into lanes, his feet

pushing down the shadow
whose patterns he becomes

while trucks, one by one,
pass him by,

headlights pouring
from his face, his eyes

cracked as the Hudson
wraps street lamps

in its rippled blue shells,
the summer's thin, thin veins

bursting with dawn,
he, now suddenly free,

from the air, from himself,
his heart beating far, far

behind him.

Flight from Houston in January

Both sides of the sky
are visible from here,

the clouds below us
and a clear blue above.

If clouds were boats,
one would row them

with rods of lightning
across the world.

In Houston, already perhaps
a thousand miles back,

for days I saw the warm
side of the sky, the sun

touched with Mexico . . .

We drop through thousands
of feet of clouds,

the wings threshing them
like cotton for quilts.

Suddenly, the white hills
of Pittsburgh . . .

I see only the dark side
of the sky

as we hit the frozen runway.
A Pan Am takes off,

leaving behind
a row of snow dervishes

whirling and whirling
till they become the trance

of everwhite trees
found on Christmas cards . . .

The trees crumble, just
so much white dust.

Stationery

The moon did not become the sun.
It just fell on the desert
in great sheets, reams
of silver handmade by you.
The night is your cottage industry now,
the day is your brisk emporium.
The world is full of paper.

Write to me.

IV

Survivor

Someone lives in my house

At night he opens the refrigerator
inhaling the summer's coriander

On Radio Kashmir he hears announced
all search has been abandoned
for last year's climbers
on Nanga Parbat

My house breaks
with the sympathy of neighbors

This is his moment

In my room
he sits at the table
practices my signature answers my mail

He wears the cardigan
my mother knit for my return

The mirror gives up
my face to him

He calls to my mother in my voice

She turns

He is breathless to tell her tales
in which I was never found

I Dream It Is Afternoon When
I Return to Delhi

At Purana Qila I am alone, waiting
for the bus to Daryaganj. I see it coming,
but my hands are empty.
"Jump on, jump on," someone shouts,
"I've saved this change for you
for years. Look!"
A hand opens, full of silver rupees.
"Jump on, jump on." The voice doesn't stop.
There's no one I know. A policeman,
handcuffs silver in his hands,
asks for my ticket.

I jump off the running bus,
sweat pouring from my hair.
I run past the Doll Museum, past
headlines on the Times of India
building, PRISONERS BLINDED IN A BIHAR
JAIL, HARIJAN VILLAGES BURNED BY LANDLORDS.
Panting, I stop in Daryaganj,
outside Golcha Cinema.

Sunil is there, lighting
a cigarette, smiling. I say,
"It must be ten years, you haven't changed,
it was your voice on the bus!"
He says, "The film is about to begin,
I've bought an extra ticket for you,"
and we rush inside:

Anarkali is being led away,
her earrings lying on the marble floor.
Any moment she'll be buried alive.
"But this is the end," I turn
toward Sunil. He is nowhere.
The usher taps my shoulder, says
my ticket is ten years old.

Once again my hands are empty.
I am waiting, alone, at Purana Qila.
Bus after empty bus is not stopping.
Suddenly, beggar women with children
are everywhere, offering
me money, weeping for me.

A Call

I close my eyes. It doesn't leave me,
the cold moon of Kashmir which breaks
into my house

and steals my parents' love.

                        I open my hands:
empty, empty. This cry is foreign.

"When will you come home?"
Father asks, then asks again.

The ocean moves into the wires.

I shout, "Are you all happy?"
The line goes dead.

The waters leave the wires.

The sea is quiet, and over it
the cold, full moon of Kashmir.

The Tiger at 4:00 A.M.

Something waits
to print on this blankness,

something still asleep
in an envelope of fur,

outside in the January snow.
I open the window:

On the slopes of Kumaon
ten thousand miles away,

in terror of the man-eater,
the peasants lock themselves in,

their huts wrapped
in a plaster of frost.

On the table before me,
the wind rustles the page.

Something begins to stir:

The villagers are coming
back to life,

the sun once again
dresses their huts.

It soaks up the dawn's
washable blues.

Something stalks through the page.

In the Mountains

Somewhere
without me
my life begins

He who lives it
counts on a cold rosary
God's ninety-nine Names in Arabic

The unknown hundredth he finds in glaciers
then descends into wet saffron fields
where I wait to hold him

but wrapped in ice
he by-passes me
in his phantom cart

He lets go of the hundredth Name
which rises in calligraphy from his palm
Fog washes the sudden skeletons of maples

Farther into the year by a broken fireplace
I clutch the shiver of a last flame
and forget every Name of God

And there in the mountains
the Koran frozen to his fingertips
he waits

farther much farther into the year
he waits for news of my death

Houses

The man who buries his house in the sand
and digs it up again, each evening,
learns to put it together quickly

and just as quickly to take it apart.
My parents sleep like children in the dark.
I am too far to hear them breathe

but I remember their house is safe
and I can sleep, the night's hair
black and thick in my hands.

My parents sleep in the dark.
When the moon rises, the night's hair
turns white in my arms.

I am thirteen thousand miles from home.
I comb the moon out of the night,
and my parents are sleeping like children.

"My father is dead," Vidur writes,
and a house in my neighborhood, next
to my parents', has burned down.

I keep reading the letter.
                    If I wake up,
my body will be water, reflecting the fire.

(for Jon Anderson)

About the author

Agha Shahid Ali divides his time between Kashmir, where he is originally from, and the United States, where he teaches in the M.F.A. Creative Writing Program at the University of Massachusetts—Amherst. His six collections of poetry include *A Walk Through the Yellow Pages, A Nostalgist's Map of America,* and *The Belovéd Witness: Selected Poems.* He is also the translator of *The Rebel's Silhouette: Selected Poems* by Faiz Ahmed Faiz as well as the author of *T.S. Eliot as Editor.* His poems appear regularly in journals such as *Antioch Review, Chelsea, Denver Quarterly, Field, Grand Street, Paris Review, Poetry, Tri-Quarterly,* and *Yale Review.* He has won fellowships from the Pennsylvania Council on the Arts, the Ingram-Merrill Foundation, the Bread Loaf Writers' Conference, and the New York Foundation for the Arts.